# SACRED THINGS

## Poems by
## Aaron Rudolph

Bridge Burner's Publishing  2002
Mankato, Minnesota

SACRED THINGS

ISBN 0-9702851-1-6
Library of Congress Control Number 2001095141


Cover painting: "And Then the Leaves" by Cassandra Labairon.

Photograph of Aaron Rudolph by Suzanne Bunkers.

The author and publisher gratefully acknowledge the attention given to this project by Roger Sheffer and Eddie Elfers.

**Bridge Burner's Publishing Company**
PO Box 5255
Mankato, MN 56002-5255
www.bridgeburners.com

*for my grandfather, Louis Rudolph,*
*who always had a story to share*

# Table of Contents

## III.  Her Words

## IV.  Making Movies

# The Night His Family Was Honest

## For Three Men Named John

### I. 1955

The truth of ambulances
escaped him for many years.
Smack in the middle of the century
he played in his yard with neighborhood kids
as a bark of an ambulance halted their game.
His mother grabbed his wrist, directed him
away from paramedics and promised ice cream,
anything to distract him from death,
a process like an inappropriate gesture.
His grandfather, the man
with his name, breathless
in an upstairs bedroom. He now only knows
this from what he pieced together.

### II. 1974

When the boy grew to a man and raised
his own family in his grandfather's house,
he saw each of his four children
dream in the very room that held
the secrets of the old man's life.
The room was passed down
like used clothes, and when his youngest son
came to occupy it, his elder siblings
spilled the tale of the room, the mystery
of death secured within the walls.

### III. 1990

The boy, named for his father, cried
and spent months sprawled on the floor
in his parents' room, the bedroom's history
too powerful to accept. He thought
of the room as a tomb and forced
himself claustrophobic, called
the room too small for two people.

## What She Said About Her Grandfather's Funeral

*for JAFR*

He was the old man
shelved in the corner
of the crowded room
alone, glancing
at the newly married couple.
He only spoke
when his daughter
asked him if he was okay.
His face, a large beach ball,
his eyes, birds viewed
through smeared glass.
His family spoke of him,
how he was still alive,
a photograph fading on a sidewalk.

So when he died
and she couldn't attend
his funeral,
she cried
because her mother cried,
the only one distraught enough
to weep over the casket.
His other children,
at the reception,
cursed through cake
about money
and the lack of a will.
And the daughter became her father,
a silent parrot
across the room,
as the others divided
his whole life
like stacks of crumpled bills.

## Mom Making Sopapillas

She came home, threw books on the table,
shook her head at teachers, movie villains
grinning with thin moustaches.
She comforted herself by pounding flour.
She weighed it with water and punched
frustration out on the growing dough,
dinner only an hour away.

In this way, she sculpted sopapillas,
the heat within her
transferred to *masa*, hands careful,
and shapes began to appear,
geometrical wonders. No formulas or equations,
only fingertips smoothing corners,
creating sopapillas. Symmetrical,
beautiful enough to display. While they fried
in grease, she wiped her forehead,
breathed in and breathed out
the odor of art. She followed this pattern
as routine and when she became a mother
she stacked the sopapillas
on top of each other
while her kids watched them wobble
in rhythm. When she turned away,
her sons snuck some and ate them out of sight,
letting the heat warm their hands and the smell
enter them, sniffing with caution,
as a wine connoisseur would.

Her family became connoisseurs of sopapillas
and with each passing year regarded them as delicacy.
Her skill was obvious from her hands,
soft as when she was a girl.

## At Grandma's

*Río Lucío, New Mexico*

Holidays often meant cousins
splashing in the Río Pueblo,
shallow water shriveling fingers
and toes. Aunts and uncles were a line
of dignitaries; they'd squeeze my shoulder
and I could feel palms warm with blood
roaming like mine. I'd say how old
I was, what grade in school,
my latest hobbies. Tradition and ceremony
and kitchen smells of beans and posole
hovered over the television. Outside
by the river, the weeds and wild flowers
waved aromas like mountain perfume
so that the odor always takes me back.
Grandma sits at the table, beckoning me with hands,
saying: *How have you been, mejíto?*

## Sacred Things

I. *Northern New Mexico*

The land that first heard Spanish tongues
in 1598, where a German-Jewish man fell in love
with a country girl named Aldelita a hundred years
ago, where my mother and father met and named
their second child Aaron, a Hebrew name
far removed from the Juans and Miguels
he played with in school. The place of history
and tradition: *luminarias* lighting
a path at night, a glowing trail
outlining this place, singing people home.

II. *Family*

When my grandfather died I couldn't cry,
my eyes an old well, water
long removed. I was fourteen and he drove
me all the way to Albuquerque,
ordered me to stay in the truck, three hours,
sitting, waiting, desert sun blowing
like a malicious god, full of spite.
Grandpa waltzed up to the truck, sweat
on his face from dancing. He hummed
and drove home, two hours, his fingers
two-stepping around the steering wheel.
He had the most glorious Spanish accent,
smooth and almost singing words:
*mejito, hombre, muchacho.*
*Grandson, home, future.*

III. *Isolation*

I cried until morning on my first night
alone in Minnesota and again
the next night. I cried so long
I forgot my pain, misplaced it

somewhere inside, behind my pancreas
or next to my liver. I mean to say
that the pain was physical, a steel ball
rolling around in my chest, forcing
my lungs weak, a gasp for air
forming an awkward melody, a beat
that captivates: chest heaving, and shoulders
shooting up and lilting down, a weeping
samba, one with music initiated
from the rhythm of emotion.

## The Night His Family Was Honest

In high school, his friend dragged him feet first
through snow and slush, drunk head
trailing behind, bumping against concrete.
Later at home, his mother cried into a coffee pot,
struggling to force caffeine down his twisted mouth
while his father stripped his clothes,
as an Army officer would bust a sergeant,
and carried him to the bathtub, the cold water
doing what the coffee couldn't do.

Then his father dressed him and walked him
around the house. His younger brother and sisters
listened to babbles about Corona and peppermint schnapps.
His little sister giggled every time he said fuck
and his mother cringed when he asked for more beer.

His father remained somber, his warm hand
on his son's neck, thoughts of strangling
him quickly fading.

## A Poem to My Niece, Almost Three Years Old

*Everything she wants she sees*
*in the dark coin of this child's eyes.*
—Valerie Martínez, "Traveler"

You count in Spanish
            *uno, dos, tres*
Just as my sister taught you.

You perform on cue
Acting as jester, arms whipping
Around like confused snakes
When your mother demands it.

You laugh and your eyes
Glaze solid like pebbles.

In your eyes I see my years
At Mora Avenue Elementary
Where I was picked last for dodge ball,

Where I kicked a ball into someone's yard
And spent three days after school
Because I climbed the fence

To retrieve it. I etched
Doodles in my Big Chief notebook,
Wrote an acceptance speech
For when I was elected President.

Your eyes also hold
The picture of a girl,
            *Elena, Elena, Elena.*

I think *muy bonita*, the same words
Your mother says at night
As she stands above you,

The Sandman with your mother's face,
Spreading a kiss like sleeping dust
Across your forehead.

## Lobo Means Wolf

Lobo is wolf, yes, but I have stories
where lobo means that and it means
my grandfather smoking a pipe in his living room,
our favorite college basketball team
battling their opponent, sometimes
honoring the Lobo with victory,
a hard-fought game, sweaty giants
bent over, hands on knees, the mountain
altitude refusing air to their lungs.

Lobo stands for me jumping, six years old
and already a diehard fan, lobo spelled
in squares with masking tape on my shirt,
the number of my favorite player
on my back. A look in the mirror
shows my grandfather has taped
a frowning face, a joke
only he laughs at. I remove the shirt
rearranging the frown into a 7. The eyes
are extra, stuck on the floor. The team
has a 7, a scrawny kid named Trason
from Mississippi. *A Southern boy,*
Grandpa laughs, *he scored all of three points
last year.* He never plays but I continue
to imitate him when I shoot dirty socks
into a make-shift basket from a hanger.

Weekend means sleepover at Grandpa's
and more Lobo games where I am
the Southerner named Trason.
In my grandparents' kitchen, 7 is lucky,
hitting the winning shot each game,
but on the screen he never plays, the team
still wins, the song "Celebration" throbs
from the television as I dance.
Grandpa laughs between puffs on his pipe.

18

## Indelible

My father's father was there for the world
on the front page of the "City Happenings" section,
knees bent and arms upward, dancing, age 77. His partner
sweating, cheeks sucked in, gulping air,
fervent to keep up. I nicknamed her Sisyphus,
rolling the rock up the hill. Keeping up with Grandpa
was as hopeless. He danced like this often, driving weekly
to Albuquerque for seniors mixers. He met women
who pinched his cheeks and pinched mine
the one time I went along for the ride. I never told anyone
about the trip, about the dancing, a promise made between
two men. Grandpa was a changed man
once he was a widower, not in drastic ways
but the photo was proof. His dancing
was nothing he talked about and it took
the Sunday paper for my father to see him
as a flash, pressed gray suit,
shoes caked with years of polish,
a story for each coat scrubbed
into the leather. The newest coats shone brightest,
even in bad lighting and on that grainy paper.

We didn't know about the picture
until our aunt told us, but our father knew,
and he looked at the wood stove when we asked
where it had gone. There, in that stove,
fire reduced Grandpa's image to ash,
his dancing burned into a memory. But still
without record, I see his hips swaying, hands
firmly on a woman's hips, his shoulders dipping
with the music, each muscle synchronous,
even his mouth, a knowing smile in step with the beat.

# Last Seat On the Bus

*Do you think that I do not love you*
*if I scream*
                    *while I die.*

—Leslie Marmon Silko, "Deer Song"

# Five Drinks into a Conversation

*for Jon G. Koch*

Together, we tried to pour things
into our heads. We discussed
literature and politics, movies and women,
and we concluded
that our conversations weren't heavy
like syrup, so they wouldn't stick.
*We're too young*, you repeated
and I circled my glass
of beer on the table,
agreeing, head down.

I've always been too young.
At ten, I realized that I'd forever
man the kids' table during Thanksgiving
dinner. I was destined to be hunched
over the small bench I first sat on at four.
The table was a battlefield
with cousin Eric kicking his brother
under the table and my sister
flicking green beans like grenades
at my ear. In the dining room, the adults
discussed issues and always sounded
like the Martians
in bad science-fiction movies.

We are those sputtering aliens
these days. You and I
laugh and shrug our shoulders.
*We'll never have answers*, we decide
as we walk away from the table
thirty minutes before last call,
only a quarter to tip the waitress.

## My Brother Sits on a Rock Overlooking the Gallinas River

There, shirtless, he looks like the Pugilist at Rest,
Thom Jones' pugilist, contemplation
laced in each muscle from forehead to jaw,
down thin biceps and tanned back. His face
leans down at the river and the trout
cannot see him, the currents rush them
away. His mind must be a thousand miles
from fish and their struggle,
though anyone can see his physical presence,
this body, its tired stance, its swimming,
the oak arms rounded up, stopping
at a fist, powerful ball, and sleeping
on it, a head, this child's face capping
off a young man's body. How did I not see
this coming? Who is he? He looked
right in his eldest brother's face and said,
*I am Chicano. What are you?*
He was fifteen and too damn smart,
the kind that's frightening and makes people
think; think about themselves and what
they are. Are their lives meaningful?
My brother sits on that rock shirtless
and has a whole life to contemplate.
His life, a highway billboard, has writing
only in the top, left-hand corner
and he has years to fill the whole thing.
Others see their billboard and it's all covered.
But he doesn't think in those terms. His life
isn't oversized paper; it's right here. Over the river
he sighs and looks intently at the dark water,
watches his reflection swim away with each wave.

## Falling in Love at the Peanut Festival

Peanuts crept everywhere! Peanuts infested
the food, slithers in the potato salad,
whole peanuts floating in the cheese dip.
Peanuts named the dances, the songs
accompanying them. The princess
who served them was a short
fidgety girl, wearing a velvet peanut glued
to a tiara waving wildly from the wind,
the applause, her excited jumping,
an odd celebratory instinct,
her boding shaking upward, shaking down.

Her sister, Deb, was even shorter
but she was more still as she stood
next to the princess for photos.
Deb was a year younger and didn't care
for peanuts, the farms that fostered
them, the town that thrived
from their growing. All her life
adults called peanuts a savior
as if they grew wings and patrolled the town
by night, evil doers fleeing from peanut's presence.
She saw how they nestled in soil,
how shells cracked when pinched
between fingers, listened to them crunch
as she chewed. She threw
the shells at her sister, let out
a guttural noise, a Caveman noise, each time
one hit the velvet peanut. Her sister,
the princess, rolled her eyes
at her and continued speaking to well-wishers.
A boy in Deb's class laughed at this
and winked at her, gave a thumbs-up
for the thrown shells. He imagined
Deb in the crown, ruler of peanuts,
flinging her empire at confused subjects.

*Aaron Rudolph*

## Reasons for Poetry

*for Valerie Martínez*

When I saw the hawk and two crows
I heard the poetry teacher
        She implored
Turn it on,  on,  on.

Poet, these birds fly for you.
They have not heard your name,
read your lines or been briefed
on your philosophies. The hawk flees
her predators. The crows peck
at the hawk, peck until she falls,
drops and plops on earth, wings smashed and spread
on the ground in hostility. The crows know
only of necessity and not art. They chase
the hawk because they must. If only they were aware
that I watch them because I must.

I see three figures gliding, three blips
on a map. Two small, one large. The small ones
gain. It's theater. I enjoy
the flutter of hawk wings, desperate, the mammoth
wing span good for power
and not speed. Crows, however, understand
speed. They are Ferraris, their feathers
glitter like chrome. The sun reflects them
in flashes and they are on the hawk in seconds.

We learn to observe the world
like squirrels watching in the distance.
squirrels will only move when forced
to do so. A squirrel can wait
out a situation. The eyes move, the body
stays sedentary. They eyes move
rapidly in a hunt of everything around it.
Observe a cardinal, a red clump

25

resting on grass and the squirrel,
a predator's lunge away. The cardinal
knows not to stand guard. There are some animals
born as natural stalkers. Also, lives the squirrel.

Poet, scribble notes, learn about the world
in your back yard. It grows. Everything
has instincts and impulses. The tree
where the squirrel lives shrinks in November.
It straightens in May. Please, take notice.
See it happen and interpret it with lyricism.
Let the images grow strong, watch closely.

## Talking by a Campfire: Mineral Hill, New Mexico

I assume I can conquer all,
that I can swim bull headed
through angry oceans. I assume
that I am strong, that I can see
through rock and that I
have Socrates' musings stuffed in my head.

Imagine how it all crumbled
when the blond kid in the embroidered Mexican shirt
exposed me as a stammering mute
when he mapped out his life,
all nineteen years of it.

After high school he packed his lucky bandana
in an exhausted hiking pack and camped out
on the highway until he got a ride to college.
When that lost its energy
he sweet-talked his way to Albuquerque
to live like the coyote and soak up
all the power of the soil.

I assumed the power resided within me,
dancing the cha-cha in my veins
but while I sat against an adobe wall,
breathing in stagnant, stale air,
this other guy was darting across
the desert discussing Nietzsche,
Mexican food and the Dodgers
with an old, trusting couple in a Plymouth
who recognized that he deserved a rest
because he was out there, he was living.

## Of Towing and Other Forms of Separation

All day I troll the lot by foot,
recording information on every car
waiting in disciplined rows. In the third grade,
Bobby Jenkins brought all 32 of his Hot Wheels
to school and guarded them with fatherly
sternness until Leroy created a diversion;
his friend rushed suddenly, as if from the earth,
and snatched the cars, several in each hand,
laughing, running, laughing, until they made it
to the dumpsters and hid, leaving Bobby crying
with the few toys left. Behind the stink
of garbage, the boys counted their loot,
sharing visions of crashing
those cars together safely behind bedroom doors.

On cold days I expect a tornado to swirl
into this lot and scoop the cars, the way Leroy's buddy did.
With a child's hand,
the tornado would grab these cars and spin away
out of sight. The cars would float. In my dreams,
faceless bodies float, and I strain to distinguish
any features. At work, I'll sometimes
squeeze my knuckles against my chest and wait for a pain
to center around my heart chamber. I don't know
that this is how loneliness feels, or how a child feels
when his passion has been ripped from him,
only that it's approximate to time on the lot
amidst old cars shapeless as bodies in dreams.

## The River They Shared

The river currents were hands
of an angry surgeon, pushing
and searching. Pounding down
on swimmers, young bodies bobbing,
weaving, struggling. A girl
yelled for her father, her head
thrashing up and down, her cries
interrupted by water filling lungs
as the currents pulled her under.
And she spit out the liquid
and *Help me, Daddy!* long enough for
people to hear and react. Her father
reached for an arm, the one limb visible,
as if detached and floating
away from her, looking for help. He clamped
his hands around her arm, so thin
he feared snapping it. He tugged until
a face emerged; her eyes were closed
and he cried for her, from his gut,
the way a singer calls for a note
to come from far inside
so that it resonates so clearly it stings.
That's how this father cried for his daughter
when he held her there, on the river bank,
her body cold and quiet,
nearly fading with the afternoon sun.

I can almost feel
the fragile body in my arms,
heavy and awkward like firewood.
He looks down at her
and stops weeping at the moment
he believes she is dead.

## Last Seat on the Bus

On all those bus trips—
1,200 miles, frozen farm land
blended into mountains, the snow
less angry with each state west—
it seemed I always got the last seat,
across from the couple from Des Moines,
he 22, she 19. They huddled tighter
with each person scooting past.

The lunch line in middle school
meant sitting in gym bleachers.
I sat alone and counted the packs
of students, devised that the average
was four kids in a group, and I
brought down the average, but
I was awful in math so I knew
my calculations were faulty.

School was like that; I thought all
classes were spoken in Russian
since I only heard what sounded
like people whispering through hands.
Science classes sounded Portuguese,
a smooth chant, almost recognizable,
almost Spanish (*Yo hablo un pequito*) but distant
enough that shock and horror filled

me when my name made the list
for Honors Science in the ninth grade.
The class clown frightened me
a little when he toppled my chair
but more when he solved equations
like connecting the dots. He was the star,
the largest ball of luminous gas.
I admired comets in elementary
and my dad, brother and I tried to locate
Halley's Comet through the telescope

that was a Christmas present. My brother
was fuzzy in the lens from ten feet
away in daylight. Everything appeared
out of focus after that, and when I got glasses
I became the blur as though everyone
viewed me through a cheap telescope.
Bus passengers understand it all
and scurry to the best seats. The last
seat is mine, the one next to the man
screaming, *Jesus loves me; I am Jesus.* Next
to the man traveling from Chicago
to Reno, three days of sweat stagnating
on his skin, an open window carries him
around the bus, wakes me up at 2 a.m.
The last seat is meant for me, the way
it stands out, the way it seems disconnected.

## Not Body

*for Connie*

I was young and frightened; girls
could sense this from me, could see
this as a physical extension of the body,
like a radioactive glow, so when
Dolores Montoya read that I was listed
as her "Most Compatible Mate" on
a Valentine's questionnaire, she mocked a gag
in front of her friends, her finger driving
toward her tongue. Their laughter circled
in the hall. I heard the whole thing from
behind a corner, bent over, a wounded spy.
Each pang of laughter resounded a little more
than the last, like being stoned
with larger and larger rocks. Such an attack
damages the body, the flesh on a person
dissolves into nothing with enough abuse,
the physical case turns to bloody scraps,
an offering for buzzards who also circle,
who swoon down with open beaks, diving
at flesh, intoxicated by the vulnerability
of fragile and helpless bodies.

Body is not a word we use,
not the word we conceive.
You carry your being
with a grace that can't be named.
You cannot be confined, what you are
does not answer to the physical. I learn this
from you without words. Without mention
of the word, your glow writes a litany.
Your presence is validated
by laughter and tears.

By the laughter and tears you share
and by those that rise from me, confused
yet glad for hearing the song you sing.

## State Street on Halloween: Madison, Wisconsin

like when during a Wisconsin fall moon
a man dressed in Halloween clown garb
    is asked, *Hey clown, can I bum*
*a cigarette?* as if the clown is the obvious choice
    for inhaling tobacco, as if
this man with last-minute-rushed-apparel
    whose very face, marred by a rainbow
of forced-smeared-on-smile is the one man
    who would carry a cigarette, as if
this clown has been driven to smoke
    by Midwestern pressures
of faking perfection and acting subdued
    by imaging what the dead feel in a coffin—

it is without question-or-any-other-doubt
that this clown is the man who has a smoke
because he doesn't laugh
at a joke about Iowa farm boys.

## Story

Alvin contemplates the difference
between Navajo and Navaho
calls both unnecessary
only words.  Labels given by others
and so he smiles in the mirror
calls himself Invincible
poses like Narcissus

watches his eyelids fall down
watches his face fade in   out
watches his nose, ridge, thick and full
and how his eyes are dark, the eyes
of his grandfather, his mother says
and so he feels stronger

and when the sun sets
the mesa brightens and the clay
sleeps like moss on the bluffs.
Alvin sees it all, telescopic eyes
focusing on the rocks up there,
the way they dull the landscape

the way his uncle talks of it
early mornings when he ambles
from his pick-up, eyes opening
to sunlight, work clothes on, balancing
coffee and donuts in both hands.

He sits with Alvin and recites
his version of the Creation Myth
how their Makers knew they'd sit here—
Alvin and his uncle—
and how they'd wonder
why the formations—
camels, warriors, sea vessels—
are only mirages, the one reason
the people do not forsake the land.

In his uncle's story
the formations are fragile,
to touch them cheapens everything,
the disrespectful act crumbles
rock to powder, destroys mystique
leaving land flat, the next village
visible all those miles away.

*Aaron Rudolph*

## When I Was Nine

These pockets
are cautious
and untrusting,
eyeing me
expecting that I
will raid them
will conquer them
for dollar bills
abducted at night
in ironic darkness
while my father
sleeps pantsless.
His money, hard-earned,
swims dishonestly
into hands
dirty and anxious
as a teen-aged boy
spying nudey magazines
merely for the chill,
the shivering of spine,
a signal away
from childhood.

## Returning to Minnesota

I dreamt that I was back in Mankato
napping on my bed, my old studio apartment docile,
a bear after winter squinting in light
and breathing air dormant for months.

After briefly waking that same night
I dreamt I was in my brother's living room,
an arena with at least ten children moving,
a movie playing, one in black & white
about astronauts, several children dressed
in shiny space suits. The whole thing is hypnotic.
I wake up.

If I had read more Freud I could connect
the two dreams, express to a professional—
or anyone crazy enough to listen—
that returning to Mankato is like orbiting the earth
waiting for a place to land; from outer space,
the whole world looking occupied.

# Her Words

*This was his passion, that only she might see. The chance*
   *He might feel some movement on her lips*
   *Toward laughter.*

—Alberto Álvaro Ríos, "Teodoro Luna's Two Kisses"

## The Lost Brother Appears in the Smoke of Burgers

*Lake Havasu City, Arizona*

The gods of misplaced brothers
showed their faces
in the bubbles of Jason's Dr. Pepper
at Burger King, gave him the sign
so that he saw his brother:
his walk, his face, his *May I take
your order?* all in the assistant manager.

Jason met his fate
the day he craved a burger.
He asked a woman mopping floors
about the freckled man, about his name,
how he might speak of his brother
in childhood, two cubs wrestling,
training for the day they'd part.

The name didn't match nor the history
and as the woman pointed out,
their faces weren't similar, the faith
of my friend's expression betraying him.
Jason knew this the whole time
and his disrespect to the gods,
watered-down soda spread on linoleum,
was meant more for the woman,
the punch of her words
too sharp not to respond to.

Aaron Rudolph

# First Rain in Three Months

*Las Vegas, New Mexico*

The drought created confusion
in the city. Men showered lawns
with bath water and police
scanned neighborhoods in slow motion,
ready to cite anyone spraying lawns,
those lavish with water
hiding behind bushes and under trees
as squad cars approached.

The community pool shut down
and chlorinated water bubbled,
the pool like a kettle, lifeguards sitting
silently, heads down, looking
at bare feet. The lack of water
the same as a lack of air.

The mayor issued water-saving measures,
called upon people's decency, their need
for water secondary to the need for order.
The city dulled in drought, greens wilted
to yellows and the golf course closed
leaving stray range balls
abandoned on islands of limp grass.

For weeks, people bought bottled water
and held it up in glasses,
marveling at its complexity
for the first time. The liquid
a healing source, the reason Poncé de Leon
went mad on Floridian beaches, growing older
as his throat coughed in deprivation.
Water wasn't youth-in-a-bottle for the town,
rather a reminder that water does not grow
in the Southwest; the rivers are confused.

After three months, it did rain
and the cracked earth darkened with wetness;
families celebrated as they would
a newborn. Some children met
in an alley with deep holes
belly-flopping in rain water,
their own pool. They caught the rain
in their mouths, swallowing slowly.

I write a poem about it fifteen years later
while it rains outside. Half finished
with the poem, I put the notebook down
and run to the backyard. My hair heavies
and my eyes are pounded with pebbles
of rain which skid off my face. I think
that I might catch a cold, but also
of those children jumping in puddles.

## Music

If it were as easy as turning on the radio
there would be no need to search
for it, to dissect words for it,
to scream at page or screen.

If finding it were as simple as breathing
or speaking or shouting, we wouldn't
praise, applaud, canonize it.

Sometimes, when it's especially well hidden,
I dare it to jump from the pen
land graceful and find rhythm,

to unify with the page, turning
mystique into the recognizable,
the unspoken into the spoken, silence
slowly spinning toward melody.

## What Minnesota is

*Mankato, Minnesota*

What it is, is the crows
darker in night, lounging on branches,
moving only for the wind. From
a quarter-mile away, these birds blend together
and it looks as if my 6-year-old niece
colored the scene herself, lost
in her thoughts, giving too many strokes of black crayon
for each branch, each crow, neglecting the pale trunk,
the glowing moon, or the almost-iridescent man
walking on a sidewalk below the tree.
His head, down and resting
on his chest (or his hands,
in an uncontrollable shake from the January chill)
isn't visible over the heavily-colored crows
weighing down branches, making no noise,
not even flying off, tired from the attention.

*Aaron Rudolph*

## Rock-n-roll Poem for a Fellow Poet

That term—rock-n-roll—has been diverted
like leaves in October, some floating
far away. The tree stands tall at a distance.
You let music seep into your lungs,
let it grow in your veins. We could say
it was part of your soul, finding its way
into your speech, your poems. A clunky rhythm
saved by a melody, all grace and ceremony.

Every time I sat in your truck
a guitar riff would carry me off
and the Midwest was no longer gray,
the sky opened and it was all so clear,
the sun visible, the moon rocking
on the other side of the galaxy,
nodding its head, an instinct
initiated by the soothing beat.

I still read your words.
I snap my fingers after each line.
Do you think Ginsberg and Kerouac
ever dreamed they were butterflies
gliding in the wind, a melody
carried by the wave of one note?

## Slick, the Family Dog, Meets His Demise on Moreno Street

The mutt my sister smuggled under her sweater
as we were leaving Grandma's house. Puppy's
head nosing through for air, his eyes dark as his coat,
eyes of a lover, making life on good looks. This mutt
eased about and yawned when people pleaded
him for tricks. He was the puppeteer of our show
from the start when my sister doused him
in river water, smoothed back the hair over his eyes
and declared, *Slick!* Her nine-year-old squeakiness
enough baptismal for a laughing father to allow
the puppy to stay, asylum from rural life
where he was the litter runt, and food for all
in only one dish left him hungry, the seven other dogs
licking their lips in satisfaction after meal time.

He lived as my sister prognosticated,
mulled around the neighborhood and yelped
to be fed. He avoided the Bulldogs and Boxers
of the block. The superstar, canine prima donna,
pampered. We were willing to serve him.
A year, maybe, his coat shone like new metal
but after that, he dulled, fewer baths
and less affection. He blended into the surroundings
like a painting on the wall.

I forgot he was around and days
would pass between meetings. I stopped bending
down to pet him and he stopped moaning
for attention. He ran further and further from home,
the prodigal dog and, then, on Moreno street
a car caught him, the bumper like a swinging foot,
the asphalt like a predator's teeth, slicing
through his rear legs. A man called my father
and after the vet, Slick hobbled in the backyard,
legs wrapped in a cast. The cast pestered
him and he tore at it as if it were overactive fleas.
He managed to rip it off daily and gangrene crawled

48

in to finish what had started on Moreno Street. I wish
I could say the whole event left me sad, but it took
a week for me to notice the dog missing
and another week to ask where he'd gone.

## Dialogue with a Turkish Man on the Greyhound Bus

*January, 1999*

Mine was the last seat. I had warmed
it for 11 hours, from Denver
to this small Nebraska town.
You sat down, polite and serene,
the smell of liquor surrounding your greeting.
A Mediterranean accent, I guessed. *I am
Turkish*, you decreed, using the same tone
I'd use if I told a banker I had a gun.

You talked loudly, your voice soothing me,
annoying the girl behind us, trying to put
her baby to sleep. You ignored the kicks
she gave the seat, talking
about American university politics.
*How are Turkish relations
with Greece?* I offered, trying to sound informed.
You talked of shady Turks in American
schools, plotting against their home
government, and I listened, glad

for conversation. Literature came up
and we discussed Turkish poets.
*Rumi lived within Turkey's boundaries,
yet no one acknowledges that.* There was no
Turkey 700 years ago and there
were no Greyhounds, either. As you left
in Omaha, I imagined me, you and Rumi,
traveling by bus from Ankara to Izmir;
you discussing political spies, Rumi
screaming we were all trapped
in a metaphor for insanity, and me asking
foolish questions about Turkey's climate.

## Like Icarus

Upon learning of Icarus,
the girl asks to hear the story over
and over, her arms stretched
wide like wings weaving
side-to-side and slowly skyward
like in the story,
the sun close enough to feel,
its heat like pounding
on the chest. She blinks
in shock each time she hears
*splash*, signaling the end
for Icarus. She asks *Why?*
and looks directly up,
her eyes scanning through the clouds.

## Her Words

This man went to sleep
every night an hour before the news,
fingers aching from pushing keys down,
ears tired from the monotonous tune
of keys slapping paper, but he loved the process,
the way words appeared on his command.
He liked that it was just him and the typewriter,
the now unattended machine silent, motionless.

He didn't think about his wife because he loved her,
and when she was alive, he never wrote,
his time spent with her. He listened
to her for years and after her death
he noticed that listening to other people
wasn't the same. He taught himself to hear her.
Everyone else sounded jumbled,
words as shrieks impossible to comprehend.

This widower talked to himself,
talked himself into writing each night
and then became silent, words transferred
from his mouth to the page held on the typewriter.
He knew better than to think the words were his,
and so after years of this, writing before bed,
a book was completed and the words on each page
were his wife's. He realized they belonged to her, because
writing them made him happy, like when after a long day,
he sat back, smiled, and listened.

## Unearthing Tomatoes

How the vines rested in soil,
as fresh as new sheets. Farmers
with delicate hands sung them to sleep,
breeze and rain, a chorus humming lullabies

and Europeans sailors were like wind
banging windows. How men bent on unearthing gold,
instead dug up tomatoes, anointed them
holy, devouring them like apples,
savoring juices trickling down chins.

The way it became staple, shipped across
the Atlantic. Blending into wanting dishes,
bland without the new discovery,
its power to excite taste buds
was reason to call it one's own,
call it custom. So when its origin
is revealed and crosses an ocean

to a once mapless place lined with tomatoes,
treasure to pluck, stems snapped like necks,
the past is transformed into stories,
sharing images of Mesoamerican farmers
as nurturers, tomato as traveler
wandering two worlds.

## From the Pages of a Brochure

This isn't a border town, not Juaréz,
down the river from El Paso. People
always talk of Mexico's beauty,
the resort spots with the mariachi bands and dancers
swaying, the clip-clap-clap of their feet
singing its own song. This is the Mexico
of movies and television. People don't drive
their cars into Juaréz. *Who knows what*
*will happen? Slashed tires, bashed-in windows?*

The children wait for people
to leave their car, stick to them until
they have their pocket change. The roads
are chunks of tar, uneven, throwing cars
with no mufflers and bald tires side-to-side
like a bully plays keep away with the weak kid's hat.
Those who do drive into the city come back
to their cars to find their license plates stolen
and a note saying: *Come to the police station.*
*We'll return your plates for a small fee.*
The car and factory fumes are everywhere.
Smells become entwined, choking,
as if all toxins form hands,
wrapping tightly around lungs.

Melodramatic, perhaps, but what can be said
when a mother slaps her daughter because
the last American she begged
didn't leave her any money.

## Instant Oatmeal: Ars Poetica

*A poem is not a pop tart.* –Martín Espada

I think about cramming my head
into a microwave, warming
it until the ideas a crispy brown,
hot. I'd set the timer for two minutes
and when I heard the *bing*, I'd shout
metaphors until they became coherent.
I'd write them down in a panic,
threatening to boil my pen
if the page wasn't filled fast enough.
I'd set my notepad on the porch,
checking it every thirty minutes
for progress. I'd even lay my tongue
on the counter, as if to cool it,
all for the sake of words served
on the page like Thanksgiving turkey,
a seemingly effortless exercise.

## Sugar Packets

This starts off tragically. The wind-blown chill
of Northern New Mexico in February. The sun
out, always out, but somehow cold; the sun, the fiery ball
not fully reflected this morning on this house,
this day. There, I gathered with my father and brothers
at my grandfather's house, one month
after the funeral: bursting flowers and real weeping.

The day went sullen. The house inside
was too quiet. The furniture slept, the appliances froze
in place and the pipes hummed softly, the creaks
less overt; the Southwestern winter weak even by its own terms.

What struck me that day was not serenity
or the tone of the empty house
or my father, the youngest child,
and how he directed his sons, signaling
to put the couch here, the dishes there,
old photos somewhere in between.

I was struck by the fifty suits hanging
in the closet. I inventoried each jacket,
each pair of pants. Inside one pair,
sugar packets. The next pair, more sugar,
and then more and more
until there were two handfuls of packets
and we were all crowded in the bedroom
each person focused on all that sugar.

A person could say that sugar in the pockets
of an old man is a cliché, that the elderly
strut around, heavied with free sugar.
Each packet in my hands lay in perspiration,
sweat beads absorbed by sugar.
My grandfather absorbed stories
the same way, and he retold them
until I had his words memorized

and could mouth the words, mimic
each anecdote as if it happened
to me.  These packets became our story,
and I like to tell it just as I remember,
a closet full of suits, sugar exploding from every seam.

## Poem for Sharmark, Age 10

*and for Nick*

He watched my roommate's confident arms
control the spoon, stirring sauce in the pan.
He saw the strong grip, power of the clenched fist,
then said: *I've never seen a man cook.*

Right then, that instant, he was the smartest
anyone could hope for, the thought clearer
than anything we could dream up.
Youth has a way of revealing genius, what's
ordinarily labeled as simple
becomes profound in context. Discovery
is its own prize. He saw a man's hands
create food, learned that power can be the energy
our hands conduct, directing
itself onto everything we touch.

That's what he taught me, the lessons
his hands held, the determination of touching
every new thing in a strange house, the experience
of seeing with hands so hungry for knowledge
that they give off their own energy,
the buzz of youth spread from item
to item: his fingertips healing the kitchen table,
reviving the coffee maker, absolving a half-eaten sandwich,
touching adults in a way poetic.
And lovely. Always lovely.

# Making Movies

## POEM

This poem was called "Aardvarks in Love"
but the damn aardvarks never even looked
at each other, and they were both loners,
anyway. This made me irrational. I saw flashes,
electricity failing, the frame of a house going light
to dark in less than a second so
the poem became "The Family Who Could Not See"
until the father lit up the old kerosene lamps,
illuminating the whole family, the dog
barking at shadows like burglars. I thought
of that burglar and his reasons for crime,
saw his wife at home, cradling her stomach, visions
of pastrami sandwiches floating around her belly.
She needed to eat, so I called it
"A Burglar Feeds His Wife." The wife found
leftovers in the fridge and fed herself.
I scratched that title, got desperate
and tried titles set in place.
"Betting on Greyhounds: Phoenix, Arizona" worked
well until I lost all my money and was too emotional
to finish the last stanza and since the poem
was less of a poem and more a rant,
I titled it like those black & white bags
of cookies at the store labeled COOKIES,
so you know you're getting cookies
and not french fries or lima beans.

## Making Movies

When I reached
through your purse for a pen
and felt the leaking water bottle,
my hands remembered the grass
from Melody Park when we'd lie there,
seven-thirty a.m., arms stretched
reaching horizontally, lumps of grass
uprooted from earth to palm.

Our days were super-8 movies
that summer, and you posed,
as if mugging for a camera.
*Action* and you'd blur into focus,
and when the dew on the grass
slid down my wrist, that was *cut*.
I swore I'd fall asleep
(right there in that park) and sleep
there all day until
the director said to do it again.

## Why I'm Not a Comedian

This morning, chewing eggs and bacon,
several years after doctors warned not to,
I attempted to tell a joke
involving two ducks and a monkey.

My father was perched at the table's front,
his arms crossed like suspicious dogs.
He squinted, strained to see, my face
a blur of unintelligible anecdotes.

Apparently, I said, humor isn't something
I have a knack for.  My dad waited—
he always said timing was everything—
waited some more, then continued eating.

## Northern California, 1995

A person goes a whole life hearing about this city or that, this
landmark or that, and so it goes with the Golden Gate Bridge and the
ideas my sister collected, her vision of this mammoth, luminous thing,
a cafeteria-line of cars cruising over it, the lights outlining a frame
winking people toward it at night, its charm alluring enough to
mesmerize a whole city, gawkers traveling its length again and again.

This is what she expected, really. I was tired and wanted sleep. *How
can you sleep?* She wanted to know. Traveling, for her, is about
being knocked over constantly and then rebounding. The sight of the
bridge, as she set it up, would be a double attack. In seconds—
flashes—the car passed the bridge. My sister looked back, then
twice more. Silent. Then: *Was that it?* I nodded what she knew.
What she expected was what she imagined from television and
stories others told her, but when she saw it, observed it from all
angles, she created her own impression, initiated her own story.

## Blue Rock

This was the rock bordered by pebbles and pine cones,
the place where we went, away from adults, alone.
Family reunions at Grandma's house, we'd sneak
up the hill to Blue Rock, a small stone past the creek
where once I fell and, pants soaked, ran frightened home.

The rock stood guard, short and solid, as I'd roam
around the trees, jumping up at branches, and groan
as I missed, my palm fanning air, a noiseless shriek—
       this was the rock!

My brother stood on the rock, yelled in baritone
pounding sticks on branches, his toughness shown.
I ducked the wobbly missiles, wiped sweat off my cheek,
smiled and laughed, dodging his attacks, I was meek.
Other times, I'd climb the trail on my own,
      this was the rock.

## My Brother's Prize

My sister, only four, raised a knife
over pigtails and flung it with wobbly precision.
That knife pierced my brother's nose,
the blade sliding through skin without effort.
I screamed, loud and shrill, a construction-site
lunch-whistle scream, and my sister stared
at the knife, from her hands to my brother's face,
her eyes straight and focused, two arrows.
My brother removed the knife
like pulling a thorn from a tire.

His nose never forgot the incident, wearing
scars as trophies.  Through arguments
or daughters' birthday parties, my brother
stands upright, fists clenched, ready
for an object to attack him,
the poorly-stitched wound puffed out,
a memory of the day he let himself relax.

Sometimes he laughs about the knife,
larger with every conversation.

## There Are Too Many *Ings* in Your Poems

*July 4, 2000*

It's that sound, that *ing*, that's as glorious
as horses clapping down a parade route
or fireworks spitting as high as clouds
or spirited nieces jumping and laughing.
*Ing*—listen to it—*ing*: the way it hugs
you like a mother does her children,
and makes it seem as if beauty
means whatever you want it to.

*Aaron Rudolph*

## Over the Blue Earth River, Early Spring

*Ron's single 1988* –words spray-painted on a bridge

It took effort to write that.
Ron—I can see him—young and impetuous,
an awkward smile covering his face
with teeth flashing, climbed down
from the bridge, took the can
of red paint and carefully wrote the words,
shaking his fist down at the river,
shouting, *You never knew me,*
*never got me.*

I think about the girl. She
could be home crying or out dancing,
lip-syncing pop songs while her friends
buy her drinks, pretending
whiskey is heart medicine.
He never took her
anywhere. He only sat
by the water and daydreamed
about the catfish swimming by.

## To Be a Stand-up Comedian

The laughs. For the laughs
　　　I'd stand
up there, a stage
in a dark room
　　　a spotlight
like a monstrous torch
burning toward me.

I'd start with jokes
about my family
　　　try to relate
to the guy at a corner table
working on his fourth beer.
For his girlfriend, alert
at his side, I'd put down men
　　　show my compassion
compare men to trees
or some new invention
I just read about in *USA Today*.

When a certain joke
went laughless, I'd
　　　insult the audience
point to a potential victim
and grill him, watch the sweat
on his neck as he stuttered replies
to my questions,
　　　label it comedy.

I'd bring up current events
　　　do the standards
like calling Congress inept,
a circus of suit-wearing monkeys
waving briefcases of confetti.

When a stagehand signaled
my time was almost done

*Aaron Rudolph*

I'd start my big closer
        culmination of theme
and deliver the final punch-line,
one last rope to grab a hold of,
        say *thank you*
lower my head, posing humble
while the claps and whistles
ushered me offstage.

## The Muscular Poet

Gets up every morning, walks
Outside and greets the dew and birds
Before the daily routine of shadow boxing
Around Dickinson. Does fifty sit-ups

Before breakfast and never goes
A whole morning without bench-pressing
Neruda's lyrics till arms are limp
And even the legs cannot withstand

Another stanza. The muscular poet
Knows better than to go too far, eats
A steady diet of the good stuff, and
Stretches each muscle separately

With a delicate touch, managing
Glass-fragile tendons without tearing them.

## Mosquitoes

We sit together on the rotting bench.
No breeze in summer. New Mexico. The air,
crisp and new, perfect for the baseball
game. Then without haste, a legion
of mosquitoes hovers over the bleachers, spraying
the field like movie war planes, bullets
spit in succession, a perfect row of predators.

We remember why we came, pull out
a can of Off, a bottle of Aloe Vera lotion,
applying them urgently, our skin finds
shades of red. The mosquitoes retreat,
mostly. One brave fellow lands on
my knuckle, assessing the situation.
I whack him with my other hand
and the bug crashes to the ground,
landing on a bed of sunflower seeds.

## Ode to My Boxer Shorts

With purple goldfish swimming
on the fabric, they are my favorite
pair. The school of goldfish bulge
eyes, perhaps aware of their placement.
I wear them in comfort
and breathe easier. I have other pairs,
like the polar bear sipping a margarita,
a gift from Aunt Trisha, the woman
who gave me a coconut monkey
for my First Holy Communion.
Then there's the pair with a flashy red racer
cruising down the speedway, *Indy 500*
written in grayed cursive. I have others
that don't speak, just stripes or polka dots.
I used to have boxers with hearts on them,
a Valentine's present from Tammy, but when she
stormed out of my apartment, I rushed
to my special boxer drawer, grabbed the hearts
and chased her, throwing the shorts at her.
I screamed, *These are yours. They're cliché.*

## An Uncle Poem

*For all my uncles*

Tío Míguel was always the cool uncle,
slapping five dollars in my palm
every time he visited, saying, *How's my man
doing?* I was eight with a Kool-Aid mustache,
grass-stained jeans with holes at the knees.
I was no man but I told my mom
I wanted to grow up to be Tío Míguel;
talk like him, thick and crusty
through his wooly mustache. He swaggered
around our house, pretending to be shocked
at the islands of toys and clothes
in my room. He taught me a curve ball
and called me the next Fernando Valenzuela. I spit
in my glove like my uncle did, talked like him
and told his jokes, repeated forbidden words
cautiously, sounds wanting to burst from my mouth
like fireworks.
        He promised to take me fishing once
but we never went. I could see it:
me and my uncle, knee-deep in the Río Bravo,
a concert of fish flying over us,
diving right in our basket.

ACKNOWLEDGEMENTS

I'd like to thank my family for always being there. Also, thank you to every teacher I ever had who said, "Go for it," and meant it whole-heartedly. To every friend I made in Mankato, Minnesota, I must say you taught me more that I can even realize. You made poetry fun and important. Thanks to Northern New Mexico for being such an unusual and remarkable place to grow up. Also, I'm grateful to Cassandra Labairon for the use of her painting on the book cover and her encouragement. And last, thanks to Curt Meyer and Bridge Burner's Publishing for an opportunity to share my voice and your belief in this book.


I am grateful to the following publications where some of these poems first appeared.

*Blue Skunk Companion*: "A Poem to My Niece, Almost Three Years Old," and "Returning to Minnesota"
*Bulk Head*: "The Lost Brother Appears in the Smoke of Burgers"
*Concho River Review*: "Why I'm Not a Comedian"
*Flyway*: "What Minnesota Is"
*Mankato Poetry Review*: "The Night His Family Was Honest"
*Plainsongs*: "Instant Oatmeal: Ars Poetica"
*South Dakota Review*: "For Three Men Named John"

**Aaron Rudolph** was born and raised in Las Vegas, New Mexico, a stop on the Old Santa Fe Trail and a town once frequented by outlaws like Billy the Kid and Doc Holliday. Aaron points to the town's fascinating past as a fertile subject matter for poetry. Las Vegas has two historical sections, Old Town and New Town. The town was home to both Hispanic families who had been living in the area for generations and newcomers from the East, some there to start businesses and others looking to raise families in the evergrowing New Mexico territory.

Aaron began writing seriously as a student at New Mexico Highlands University. After graduating, he enrolled in the MFA program in Creative Writing at Minnesota State University in Mankato, Minnesota, earning his degree in 2000. Individual poems have been published in *Flyway*, *South Dakota Review*, *Concho River Review* and other magazines. Aaron now lives in Albuquerque, New Mexico.